SCIENCE TOOLS

Susan Canizares
Betsey Chessen

Scholastic Inc.

New York • Toronto • London • Auckland • Sydney

Acknowledgments
Early Childhood Consultant: Ellen Booth Church
Literacy Specialist: Linda Cornwell

Design: Silver Editions
Photo Research: Silver Editions
Endnotes: Susan Russell
Endnote Illustrations: Ruth Flanigan

––––––––––––––––––––

Photographs: Cover: Ken Karp; pp. 1–12: Ken Karp.

ISBN 0-439-04603-3
15 16 17 18 19 20   08   03

These are science tools.

Here is a funnel.

It is for pouring.

Here is a ruler.

It is for measuring.

Here is a magnifier.

It is for looking.

Here is an eyedropper.

It is for adding.

Here is a scale.

It is for weighing.

And here are pencils for writing it down.

SCIENCE TOOLS

Science tools Scientists need to measure carefully, observe closely, and record their results. They use tools to help them do these things. When you work like a scientist, you need to know how to use these tools, too.

Funnel A funnel is cone-shaped. It has a small hole at one end and a big opening at the other. Funnels allow you to pour something, usually a liquid, without spilling. For example, if you want to pour water into a bottle with a narrow spout, you put the small end of the funnel into the bottle. Then you can easily pour the water into the wide opening of the funnel. The water goes down through the narrow part of the funnel and into the bottle. This could be very hard to accomplish without the funnel. When scientists work with liquids and chemicals, measuring precisely is important. Spills and extra drops could ruin the results of an experiment. Chemicals can also be harsh. You need to use a funnel and pour with care!

Ruler A ruler is one of the tools that scientists use for measuring. This girl is measuring the length of a leaf. She might be comparing its size with that of another kind of leaf as part of a science experiment. A ruler can also tell you how tall a person is, how wide an earthworm is, or how far you can throw a ball. Rulers measure length or distance in inches and centimeters. Scientists use tools to measure carefully so that they have accurate data.

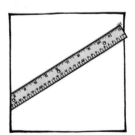

Magnifier A magnifier, often called a magnifying glass, is a tool that scientists use to make things look bigger. When you look at something through a magnifying glass, you can see details that you might not be able to see with just your eyes. Each tiny spine of the feather the boy is observing has a very small row of soft hairs on each side, almost like another miniature feather. Look through a magnifying glass to see this for yourself!

Eyedropper An eyedropper is a tool that is useful when you need to measure very precisely. With an eyedropper, you can add a liquid drop by drop. Squeezing the rubber end of the small glass tube releases the liquid a little bit at a time. The girl in this picture is adding food coloring to the bowl of water and observing the effect of each drop as it swirls out and diffuses to color the water. You can try this experiment yourself. In some experiments, just a few drops of a chemical create a reaction—too many drops wouldn't work.

Scale Scales measure weight. This boy is using a scale that balances. In the tray on one side of the scale is a large rock. When he adds just the right number of small rocks on the other side, the scale balances. This means that the things in the two trays weigh exactly the same amount. Many dry substances are measured this way.

Pencils An important part of the scientific method is to write down information. Scientists record their observations, questions, experiments, their results (the data), and what they learned (the conclusion). In this way, they can look back over their work and see how one question can lead to a new observation, how a discovery can prompt a new experiment, and how the conclusion from one experiment can lead to a new question. Pencils are the perfect science tools for this job!